My Crazy World of Football Poems

Darryl Ashton

ISBN-13: 978-1533593436
ISBN-10: 1533593434

Acknowledgements: Special thanks go to Kieran Chapman of Bumble Print, Durham, UK, who has put this book together. Without his valuable help – this book wouldn't be possible. Also, special thanks go to the editor of the O-posts football website Omar Almasri. Omar very kindly displays my football poems on his website of O-posts. All the poems in this book are the copyright of Darryl Ashton. No unauthorised copying of any items in this book is permitted without permission from the author.

About the Author...Darryl Ashton:

Darryl Ashton is now medically retired, but he was a silver service Restaurant Manager where his skills took him to land a job on the QE2. He is single, and has no children - well, none that he knows about!

He is a very keen writer, mainly of poetry, covering all kinds of topics; including, humour and more serious writings too. He thrives on political satire, and is equipped with a fantastic, and very wicked sense of humour matched with an incredible imagination.

Darryl also does stand-up comedy poem performances and is involved with various charity work. At one time, he raised an incredible £50,000 just by reading his own poems. His poems have also won several major competitions and he is also a leading reader of poems at various poetry groups on the Fylde Coast, Blackpool, Cleveleys and Lytham, all in the sunny and very friendly borough of Lancashire.

Darryl is originally from Great Harwood, a little town on the border with Accrington and Blackburn. He is a keen teller of jokes, and writing just about anything that takes his interest. Darryl says he's a late starter - he has been writing his poetry for only five years! And he's only just got to grips with his computer.

One really surprising thing that happened to Darryl was receiving an invitation from Her Majesty the Queen, to go to Buckingham Palace to actually meet the Queen where she complimented him on his poems and his fundraising efforts. Darryl also won first prize in a world-wide Elvis Presley poem competition which was organised by Graceland - Darryl was invited to Graceland where he performed his prize-winning poems featuring Elvis Presley. Darryl is also due to appear on Britain's Got Talent this year as a stand up comedian and a comedy poet.

This is Darryl's second book of poems - which includes a vast selection of his own poems. From political satire, comedy, spiritual, gospel, romance and all other kinds of poems. There's even a grand selection of comedy scripts featuring Abbott and Costello, Fawlty Towers...The Return! There really is something for everyone in this fascinating book of poems. It is a must-have book for anyone who loves poetry. Please be warned: Once you pick this book up and start to read it - you won't want to put it down again!!!!

There now follows a fascinating selection of football poems featuring teams from decades long ago. From the 60s up to the present. Some of the characters featured in this book of football poems are the meerkat TV puppets – Aleksandr Orlov, Sergei and Oleg. Also featured is the brilliant Alf Garnett and Marigold! I hope you enjoy the football poems you are about to read. The poems in this book have been blended with satire and rather 'eccentric' humour – the poems are so very different from what you would normally read – and will seriously entertain you from start to finish. Who says you can't put satire into football poems!!!! Happy Reading. And...Game On!!!!

THE CLOSING SEASON OF WORLD
FOOTBALL

The football season is
closing, and the teams
are doing battle – with
their own salvation,
Some are fighting
relegation – some are
hoping for promotion.
All over Europe – be it
France, Spain or
Germany,
Even in Italy – they
start their football
journey.

The highs and lows
of the football clubs,
Some are celebrating
in the pubs.
But some are in tears
as they face their
greatest fears,
Being relegated – it all
ends up in tears.

In Europe and beyond –
football is the game,
In America they also
play it – soccer is the
name.
For every boy wants

to be a brilliant football
star,
And if they do keep
on winning – they know
they've WON the war!

And let's not forget
the managers – who
really are stressed out.
Constantly making
their decisions – even
if in doubt.
The fans too play a big
part – they cheer their
team to win.
And then they go to
the bar – for a swift'
large tasty GIN!

I have NO doubt that
in my mind the game
is all about money.
And the English Premier
League – is the league
of milk and honey.
It is were the money
really is – and every
team wants to be there.
But you really have to
be brilliant – the money
is the lure!

There is great wealth
in the football game –

this is oh so true,
There's a lot of
entertainment – for me
and for you.
The season is a long
one – and players do
get injured.
But they always do
recover – and play on
so unhindered!

So, who will be promoted?
and who will be relegated?
The moment of truth is
closing in – it soon will be
decided.
Good luck to all the teams
who are fighting for their
lives,
Always have faith – and
say a prayer – and you
may get a nice surprise!

Good luck to everyone of
you – I mean that all so
true.
There are quite a few clubs
struggling – but soon you'll
feel brand new!
The end of the season is
fast approaching – let the
battle now commence.
The joys of 'WORLD FOOTBALL'
– is full of excitement and
suspense.

HAPPY 25th BIRTHDAY TO SKY SPORTS

Happy Birthday to Sky
Sports,
You show all sports and
of all sorts.
The football world is shown
to us,
Through a box – and cutting
the fuss.
Happy Birthday to Sky
Sports.
But I will never wear my
shorts!
The English Premier
League does shine.
On Sky Sports as some
do whine.

There are pundits galore,
getting well paid.
But why aren't they all
managing – are they
afraid?
Sky do dominate that's
for sure.
Paying huge money they
know it's a cure.
But beware dear people –
you'll pay for sure!
The bosses are cheering
their birthday today.
Happy 25th birthday – to
you today.

But what surprises have
Sky Sports got planned?
What I really should doing
is watching; Grandstand!!!!!
Here's a surprise for all
our subscribers,
We want more money –
and lots of new TENERS!
Yes, the monthly fee is
now going up.
Maybe we should sign a
football prenup!
A birthday party for the
bosses,
But sometimes they do –
count their losses!

Happy Birthday to Sky
Sports.
Another 25 years – in
cavorts.
But the fee just keeps
rising – and some folk
have left.
Feeling 'ripped off' – and
so bereft.
It's all about money –
and power and greed.
Happy Birthday to Sky
Sports – I mean that
indeed!

LEICESTER CITY: THE CHAMPIONS OF THE ENGLISH PREMIER LEAGUE

There is a football team

in the English Premier
League,
They are defying all the
odds – causing so much
intrigue.
They've hardly lost all
season long,
They're at the top –
where they do belong.

Defying all the odds,
and playing at their
best,
Every game they play –
they rise up to the test.
They play just like a
dream – and play with
skill and more,
And all the fans applaud
them – especially when
they score!

They really are the envy,
of the other football
clubs,
They are second to none,
they even have super

subs!!!!
They play to a packed
house – and their football
is a delight,
Everyone does their bit –
with winning in their
sight.

The manager has done
a remarkable job, what
a team they are.
They've won most of
their games – and now
they will go far.
A dream of dreams is
all too clear, and the
trophy they do chase.
Sitting firmly on the
top – their position
they do embrace.

A remarkable season
they have had – as
they enter the final run.
And moving ever closer –
to being the Number
ONE!
Sitting there as proud
as punch, they show us
all intrigue,
May I present Leicester
City – the champions of
the English Premier
League

THE BRILLIANCE OF ACCRINGTON
STANLEY

Well done to Accrington
Stanley, you really are playing well,
And sooner or later – in
Division One you will
surely dwell.
Your rise up Division
Two is absolutely
remarkable,
Now winning deserved
promotion – is now
very possible.

The manager has
done wonders – and
so has the owner,
All the players are
fabulous – always
shoulder to shoulder.

Out on that football
pitch – and playing
super footy,
Then come half time –
they enjoy a 'BIG' mug
of tea!

But what is their
secret, of their players
playing like silk?
'That's right. You've
guessed it – they're

still drinking all that
milk!!!!

It is obviously working,
the players are all
transformed.
They're playing better
than ever – a super
team, they've formed.

Accrington is a small
town – but it has a
fabulous football team.
Climbing up the Division
Two – it really is a
dream!

Let's all applaud them.
as they march on to
win promotion;
'The brilliant Accrington
Stanley – they play with
such devotion.'

I wonder what food they
eat – or, is that a BIG
surprise?
'I bet they go to the
market – and buy some
Oddies pies!'

Oddies pies and milk,
blimey, no wonder
they're playing well.
Just keep this up you
lads, you hear, the

pies and milk does
gel!

The fans are all behind
you – as so is the
whole of Lancashire.
And when you win
promotion – this moment
you all will treasure.

I know I speak for the
whole of Accrington –
as it is the truth, you
see;
'Let's tell the world of
a super team – the
brilliance of Accrington
Stanley.'

THE LOWER ECHELONS OF
ENGLISH FOOTBALL

Blackpool football club
are trying their best,
To play good football –
and pass the test.
They slowly climb up
the very high table,
Winning some games –
and now they are
stable.

The Oyston's won't
buy and spend any
cash,
This causes friction –
even a rash!
The fans aren't happy –
that is true,
They voice their anger
at the privileged few!

Little Fleetwood Town,
they've slipped up.
They've lost their form
and won't win the cup.
They did play well – and
won each game,
But now they're struggling –
who is to blame?

They are close to the
bottom – and they do
fear,
But they'll start winning –
and then we'll all cheer!
They started so well –
but now they do struggle,
But, they'll get better –
they're just in a muddle!

But the team doing well,
is Accrington Stanley,
In Division Two – they
sit there patiently.
They are playing well –
and that is so true,
Fans turn up – and there's
always a queue!

Two players sent off – but
the team rallied round.
They played their hearts
out – holding their ground.
Drinking their milk – it
does them all good.
They are winning more
games – as they know
they should.

The lower league's are
doing good – and deserve
a mention.
They play good football –
it is a suggestion.

Their aim is to win – and
hopefully win promotion.
Then all the fans can sing
the tuneful; 'locomotion!'

So hail the lower teams
who are paid so much
less.
Some have other jobs –
and part time, I do guess.
They are entertaining –
that is for sure.
They all want to win –
run around, and score!

THE PROBLEMS AT MANCHESTER
UNITED

The reign of Louis Van
Gaal, is now almost over,
Does this mean Jose
Mourinho – will almost
certainly be in clover?
The fans have all had
enough – and Louis
Van Gaal fears his reign
is now all over.
So will Van Gaal be on
the ferry – departing now
from Dover!

The Manchester United
board have now made
their BIG decision,
Will Van Gaail now be
ousted – by the Man
United inquisition!
He tried his best but
it wasn't enough,
Time will now surely
tell – if Van Gaal has
lost the stuff!!!!

The ending is now nigh,
as a new messiah, they
now hunt.
Who could that person
be? Is a "SPECIAL" one

in front?
I know they still miss
Ferguson – and they'd
love to have him back;
'But a very "SPECIAL"
personality – is about to
have a crack!'

Enter Jose Mourinho –
who used to be boss
at Chelsea,
Maybe he will relish
the challenge – we'll
all have to wait and
see!

He brought success to
Stamford Bridge, that
we all know well.
So will he take over
at Man U – and success,
they may all dwell.

The football world is
a rocky one – and always
full of surprises.
Sackings and signings –
all come in all sorts of
disguises.
But there's always the
mega money – that goes
with all the winning;
'And even in the news
media – the gossip they
are all spinning!'

Manchester United have
struggled – they've really
found it hard,
I bet all those players
have trained well – even
in their own back yard!
Their glory years have
halted – but this they all
do know;
'Can the "SPECIAL" one
save Man U – in the form
of Jose Mourinho?'

WHAT IS HAPPENING AT LIVERPOOL
FOOTBALL CLUB?

Liverpool football club, have
now got so very greedy,
They should be reducing
their tickets – for the poor
and the needy.
To make a quick buck or
two – which is what they
all do think,
But hiking up the costs
again – can cause a great
"BIG" stink!

The fans walked out on
Liverpool – showing their
disgust.
Walking home in anger –
their bad tempers they
did thrust.
The ticket prices now have
rocketed – not only at
Liverpool –
Why are they doing this –
do they think it's cool?

Yes, they pay high wages,
and the price of tickets
cover this;
'But some of us live in
poverty, not a life of bliss!'
I bet there are other clubs –
who are doing the same.

They really should reduce
their tickets – and stop
causing such a shame.'

Football is a business, but
greed has grasped a hold,
Hiking up the price of
tickets – they do need to
be told.
Is it too late? Will Liverpool
fans forgive?
The cynical move by the
Liverpool club – the fans are
not to give!

But, why is there all this
greed, in the name of football?
Greedy directors – and even
agents – they all hear the
money call!
A good day out for the family –
what no one can afford.
The inflated prices to see a
match – and they want us all
on board!

'So, please, you greedy football
clubs – think about your fans,
Not everyone earns mega-money –
and can sit in luxury, in the stands.'
'Please, reduce your ticket prices –
and don't act like greedy MPs;
'Or sometime in the future – you'll
be 'capped' to a "ticket-price"
"FREEZE!"'

THE JOYS AND PLEASURES OF
PREMIER LEAGUE FOOTBALL

The English Premier League
is full of woes and more,
All the classy footballers –
want to really score.
On the pitch they flash their skill –
and also their anger,
Especially those strikers –
In my day it was called:
'goal-hanger!'

Even on a crisp cold day
they always wear their
gloves,
And all the fans upon the
stands – they're chanting
in their droves.
The manager's are in their
dugout – looking so bemused,
Glancing at their substitutes –
will any of them be used?

There is also BIG MONEY in
the beautiful game of ours –
As all the Premier footballers
all drive their flashy cars.
They all work hard and play

hard – and they enjoy a beer
in the pub.
They also enjoy their dancing –
in a London' West End
"erotic-style" night club!!!!

Their career is a short one –
so they have to earn their
money,
and if they are all married –
they give money to their
honey.
Some do go off the rails –
that is a fact.
but most of the footballers
always play with tact.

Sometimes there is trouble,
and bad language is a
concern.
So if you want to "EFFING"
swear a lot – please do wait
your turn!!!!
There is also discipline – and
the punishment is tough.
Then the manager's ask their
players; 'have you had enough?'

Yes, they also spit a lot – and
it doesn't look so nice.
But that's because of the bad
taste – of their smelly' Old Spice!
They run around like cattle –
as they chase the ball;
'Scattering here – and over

there – as they hear the call.'

On occasions they do dive a
lot – to try and "CON" the ref.
Just to get a free kick – or a
penalty; 'they hold their breath!'
They run up and down the pitch –
fighting for the ball.
And when they lose their temper –
they feel a angry call!

Other countries too – they do have
super players.
I wonder before every game;
'do they all say prayers?'
"Help us lord to grasp this game –
and no kicking on the shin.
All we want to do today – is
hopefully always WIN!"

Then they are ready – and able
to play first class;
'But due to the slippery grass –
some fall on their AS*!!!!'
They've heard the call from
the lord – who shouts his
orders true;
'Go and tackle them – you swabs –
as he badly needs the loo!'

The teams are on the pitch –
as the ref does introduce.
'They cannot wait for halftime,

to drink their orange juice.'
The game of footy is a good
one – full of wacky surprises.
But why do they still kiss each
other – to express their own
vices?

No matter where in the world,
you play your football match,
The game is always better –
when you start from scratch.
Enjoy the English Premier
League – on a cold and wet
Saturday,
And when your team score a
goal – you can all shout…
HOORAY!!!!

JOHN TERRY: SHOULD I LEAVE – OR
SHOULD I CALL THEIR BLUFF?

My name is John Terry,
and I really have had
enough,
I want to leave Chelsea
football club – 'or do I
call their bluff?'
I came here when I was
fourteen – or, somewhere
in between,
I want to see the world –
if you know what I mean!

Stamford Bridge has been
my home for such a very
long time,
I've played a lot of games
here – I've seen changes
so sublime!
I want to go to pastures
new – and enhance my
skills even more;
'I'd like play till I'm fifty,
blimey, now that I will
adore!'

I have played alongside the
best – and seen some new
faces,
We always get together –
and have a bet on the races!

We all train very hard – we
do have such high standards.
If we win our game – we
have a drink afterwards!

We have a new owner – he
spends a lot of money.
He buys all the best talent –
never no one phony!
Sadly, we lost Jose Mourinho –
he left the club he loved.
But the players rebelled
against him – so out the
door he was shoved!

I am leaving after this season,
but I have to now move on.
To proudly march forward –
Maybe play football in the
sun!
I don't want an English club –
a change is what I need.
I want to broaden my
horizons, a change from the
English Premier League!

Maybe I can join my mate,
my good friend Frank Lampard.
He plays in America – and
he also plays so hard.
Maybe that's my destiny –
to America, I may go?
Playing along side Frank
Lampard – we could put on a
show!

My time at Chelsea is now
all over – time for pastures
new.
I'm not getting any younger –
but this I always knew!
I have also played for England,
and scored a good few
goals.
I also did captain Chelsea –
I was proud – and it always
shows!

I leave Chelsea football club,
with my head held high;
'Another chapter in my life,
this I can't deny.'
Will I go to America? Or,
will I stay in the UK?
Maybe I'll go to Spain – or
somewhere far, far away!

I fancy getting some sun –
Dubai would be nice.
But they aren't BIG on
football – so maybe I'll
think twice!
No matter were I go – it
will be a brand new start
for me;
'I'm leave Chelsea football
club – my name is; 'John
Terry".

JOHN TERRY: THE DILEMMA OF
A CHELSEA FOOTBALL PLAYER

My name is John Terry,
and I can't make my
mind up –
I want to play for
Chelsea – and win the
Premier League Cup.
There has been some
speculation – if I'm
leaving London town,
But I really don't know
what to do – and I wear
a frown!

I played alongside
Drogba – and my good
friend, Frank Lampard;
'When we had baths
together – we'd wear
a leotard!'
I really don't know
what to do – my career
is almost over!
I want to stay at Chelsea –
and feel all in clover.

My wages are NOT an
issue – but a pay rise
would be nice.
And playing on the footy
pitch – smelling of Old
Spice!!!!

I wouldn't mind a pay
rise – maybe £300.000
per week.
But if I asked for that
amount – it would be a
bloody cheek!

I have to consider my
future – and my family;
'Maybe I can go to division
two – and play for
Accrington Stanley!'
No, they don't need me –
they are dong well,
Maybe I can go to
Fleetwood Town – I'm
sure I would gel.

Or maybe even Blackpool –
and help them to climb
the league,
it really would be a
challenge, and create lots
of intrigue!
But, there is just one big
problem – they can't afford
my wages.
I could play for free – but
I've not done that in ages.

I want to go to the sun,
somewhere were it's warm,
Play my footy in the sun,
and use my cockney charm!

I could play for Dubai – for
the Arabian knights,
And meet old Alibaba – and
hail their footy rights!!!!

I have loved my time at
Chelsea – but my future is
now in doubt.
I will consult my agent – he
is a talent scout!
Whether or not I do leave,
my beloved Chelsea FC,
And move to pastures new –
all will be revealed on the
news – especially on TV!

I have to make a decision,
as I am now getting old.
But, like a lot of other
players; 'I hate doing what
I'm told!'
'Will I say goodbye?' 'Or,
will I stay at Chelsea?'
'It all depends what's on the
table – "mega wages", all
for me!!!!'

WHAT HAS HAPPENED TO
MANCHESTER UNITED?

What has happened to
Manchester United?
Their once brilliant play
has since departed!
From the days when
they were so brilliant,
Now they are struggling –
and it shows, so evident.

Louis Van Gaal is now
under pressure,
To start winning games,
and to reassure.
The stars of today are
all well paid,
But their skills on the
pitch – sometimes does
fade.

Wayne Rooney, is
suffering to,
He has to improve – or
retire with the crew.
Other players too – must
come together,
Support their manager –
who's at the end of his
tether!

Old Trafford should be

buzzing with trophies to
show,
But at this moment – they
all do feel low.
What can they do? What
is the answer?
How can they win – their
sparkle – to recapture?

The media are watching –
that is for sure,
Winning their games – is
the right cure.
To come together – and
play like they can,
Play for their manager –
Van Gaal, is their man.

They are suffering now –
and time is the boss,
All their talent – is it a loss?
They must improve – and
start to win;
'Or their manager is out –
that is a sin.'

Other teams too – they
also do suffer,
The winter is harsh – they
must back each other.
To reproduce their glory
days –
But at the moment – they're
all in a daze.

The Busby babes – now
they were good,
And, even Ron Atkinson –
tall, he stood!
But Alex Ferguson, he
was the master,
Winning trophies galore,
avoiding disaster!

Several owners have
cause for concern,
American's now – money,
they burn.
The Glazers are sweating –
as the pay role is gigantic,
Watching their future – the
buck is erratic!

Louis Van Gaal, he sure
is sweating,
Maybe Old Trafford is now
all fretting.
Just have more faith – and
believe in your team;
'And victory will come – you
know what I mean?'

We wish you luck and you'll
all come through,
Old Trafford will buzz – I
mean that so true.
Good luck to Man United,

I say that with a smile;
'Let's all back their manager,
Louis Van Gaal.'

BLACKPOOL vs WEST HAM -
A RE-CREATION

Come on you players' you can do it,
Said manager Ian Holloway.
Go out there and do your stuff,
Run around and act real tough!

As the ref did blow his whistle loud,
All the singing came from the crowd.
This really was a joy to hear,
Come on you Blackpool get in gear.

Crainey and Evatt passed the ball,
Then slipped it to Ince, who heard the
call
Then passed the ball to Taylor-Fletcher,
Who slot it home right past the keeper!

Then off again they did go,
Looking again to score more goals.
Stephen Dobbie controlled the ball,
And 'hammered' it in – to the open goal.

Then Philips ran with the ball,
He heard a shout: 'Hey, pass the ball?'
Philips looked up and saw Ormerod
close,
Passed it to him – and Ormerod
scores!

Blackpool are now 'two-nil' up,
And they are playing like a Premier
Club.
The hammers themselves have been
out played,
Now Blackpool can venture on their
victory parade!

What a team, and what a game,
But credit to the players – what a
dream.
But the man in charge and who changed
the club,
Is Ian Holloway – who's down the pub!

A TICKET FOR THE MATCH

My boss sent me an E-mail
I haven't answered yet.
I'm sure it was important,
As important as they get.

My boss will not be happy,
He'll foam, he'll fume and
glower,
But I've a ticket for the
match
That kicks off in an hour.

"You ought to do some
shopping,"
Calls out my irate wife,
"There's nothing left for
us to eat,
No bread, no cheese, no
rice.

We need some fruit, we
need some veg,
Some eggs, some milk,
some flour,
But I've a ticket for the
match
That kicks off in an hour.

I glance at the newspaper,
It's full of tales of woe:
War in Iraq, knife-attacks,
Share prices sinking low.

I know we should protest
and do
Whatever's in my power,
But I've a ticket for the
match
That kicks off in an hour.

I'm out the house and in
the street,
I'm rushing to the ground,
My pulse-rate's shifted up
a gear,
My heart's begun to pound.

Looks like a storm's about
to break,
Overhead thick, dark clouds
lower,
Still, I've a ticket for the
match
That kicks off in an hour.

A streetwalker waylays me
And gives me the glad eye.
Says: "Come up to my
boudoir, pal,
I'll show you a real good
time."

Now, the prospect's quite
inviting,
She's pretty as a flower,
But I'd much rather see the
match
That kicks off in an hour.

At last I'm at the stadium,
I'm all set to go in,
Then, the steward checks
my ticket,
Then informs me with a
grin…

"I'm sorry, mate, you're
somewhat late,
Perhaps your watch is
slow,
This match you bought a
ticket for
Kicked off an hour ago!"

ALEKSANDR ORLOV AND SERGEI
PLAY MEERKAT FOOTBALL

My name is Aleksandr
Orlov, and I am now
a meerkat footballer,
I cannot play in the
goal – because I need
to be taller!
I will be the referee,
and Sergei will be in
goal –
Oleg will be meerkat
striker – but he cannot
get the ball?

We are playing in the
England – in the English
Premier League –
Where all the footballers
are very rich – I have
to join indeed.
Playing also in the USA –
and scoring lots of goals,
Sergei is no good – he
always has to crawls!!!!

But, we are the meerkat
professionals – and we
have to play the same,
But if I do not score any
goal – Sergei I will blame.
Off we run onto the pitch –
it is so real grass,

But Sergei looks so daft
in shorts – he's such a
silly ass!!!!

We like the O-Posts –
super blog – they like our
writing friend,
Hello to Sir Darryl Ashton –
he writes a brand new
trend.
We love to play in America –
we feel like movie stars,
But Sergei tries to kiss me –
when I'm watching the
Star Wars!!!!

We also play the soccer – in
sunny Africa –
I run all over the hot land –
we need to drink more
water.
The Meerkat's will play
England – for a silver solid
cup,
But Oleg cannot play today –
he is just a pup!!
Sergei thinks he's the best –
I let him down gently –
He's too old, and far too
slow – he used to run so
speedy!

We have to get real – and
we cannot play the soccer –

We leave that to the humans –
then I give them all a lecture.
Sergei likes the football – and
he plays with his furry pimple –
Now he watches on meerkat
TV – it's all incredibly SIMPLE!!!!

We have to be professional –
and not act like we're smoothies,
Being in the English Football
Premier League – is better
than Hollywood Movies.

We do not like to kiss each
other – we shake our claws
to celebrate –
It just doesn't look right –
Sergei knows his fate!!!!

We will always be the better
team – but Sergei is now a
slob;
'Being in charge of IT – and
playing his computermabob!!!!'
So, now we watch the football,
on large screen television –
Welcome to meerkat football –
now it's intermission!!!!!!

MANCHESTER UNITED IN
CRISIS

Manchester United aren't
doing too well,
This is evident – as one
can tell.
Louis Van Gaal is now
under pressure,
Will the players respond –
for good measure?

They are now struggling,
to win their matches –
This has prompted an
Old Trafford crisis.
The players are not as
good as they were,
They all get well paid –
so, do they care?

It is the season to be

festive,
But the players do note;
'will they forgive?'
Will Louis Van Gaal be
sacked by the owners?
Then Manchester United
will seek Mourinho's
favours!

The gossip is rife – as
the blues march on –

Will Manchester United
recruit the 'special one?'
It's a funny old world at
the moment in football,
Will Jose Mourinho get
the call?

The Premier League is
so full of footballing
woes,
Football managers' are
sacked – anything goes!
'Why do the players rebel
like they don't give a hoot?
They should all be told;
'or they'll all get the boot!'

There seems to be friction
between some players,
Is this when the player's
all discuss their careers?
It seems no one is exempt
from getting the boot,
But, they don't seem to
care – with all that loot!

One manager will go –
another will arrive,
I think that football will
no doubt survive.
Fear not says the ref –
for he's in sole charge;
'That is a 'foul' – not a
'shoulder-like' barge!'

Welcome to the world of
football my friends,
It is here were you'll see
whole new trends.
My players aren't playing,
what shall I do?
Just wait for your fate;
'by the boardroom crew!!!!'

JOSE MOURINHO – SACKED A WEEK BEFORE CHRISTMAS

'Twas the week before Christmas,
and Chelsea are doomed,
Sacking their manager – Mourinho,
they fumed!

The boardroom were ruthless,
he has to go,
And off he went – the prodigal
Mourinho!'

The 'special one' just gazed
as he was read the last rites,
But he didn't care – it wasn't
a surprise!

A lady physio – was jumping
for joy,
She'd won her battle – Jose,
to destroy!

The players all wept as they
lost their hero,
Jose Mourinho – they called;
'Captain Nemo!'

'The Chelsea club was now
in trouble,
Who would help them? They're
trapped in a bubble!

The blues are definitely all

singing the blues,
But why are they all dancing –
on hearing this news?'

The boardroom will pay him
a massive big fee,
But Mourinho shrugs it all off –
and heads home for his tea.

'Chelsea are chasing a guy
called; Van Gaal,
From Manchester United –
will he hear their call?'

The game of football is so
full of woes,
Anything is possible – anything
goes!

The special one is no more –
as he heads out the door,
His mega fat wages – Mourinho,
does adore.

The owners have seen the
last of him now;
But Mourinho will be chuckling;
'he's the special one', somehow!'

The players are gathering to
meet their new gaffer,
But who should come in – with
a clank and a clatter!

Yes, Mourinho is Santa – he
shouts: 'Ho! Ho! Ho!

He's now gone to Lapland
with his elves, well in tow!

He turns to Chelsea and grins
like a king,
With ten million quid – oh, I will
wear some bling!

So now it's all over – It's
goodbye to Chelsea;
'Will they play better – we'll
just wait and see!'

'Merry Christmas I say – as I
feel no dismay;
'I've got "ten million pounds"
– "hip-pip"…hooray!!!!'

ENGLAND – THE UNDERDOGS
OF EURO 2016

England are the underdogs,
that is plain to see,
They're in the Euro 2016 –
and Rooney's hurt his knee!
We never seem to do well –
and we never win a trophy,
Will we win this competition –
and revel in the glory?

We all stick together, and
play our very best,
But, sadly, as we all do know –
we always fail the test.
We are manged by Roy
Hodgson – who is always
in command,
But on occasions we do
play naff – and he grabs
us by the hand.

We only just qualified –
that is the shocking
truth,
So, if we do ever win a
game, we may feel so
uncouth!
We are to play Wales,
the country of song and
voice,
But if England do beat

them – the world will
all rejoice!

We must be all positive –
and hail the England
football team,
But, sadly, at the moment –
winning is just a dream.
Maybe we can enlist some
help – especially for free;
'How about little Fleetwood
Town – or even Accrington
Stanley!!!!'

England need to concentrate
and be more positive,
Our cynicism they will
forgive.
Take each game as it
comes – like the side of
1966,
They should look to the
future – there is no quick
fix!!

We must play like we are
"world class" – and hold
our heads up high,
Because if we fail again –
we'll all be hung out to
dry!!!!
Our manager's, too, they
need to pick all the very
best players,

Or, we'll end up like Paul
Gascoigne – it'll all end in
a flood of tears!

So, come on you England –
do your duty, do it for the
Queen,
Go to Euro 2016 – show
everyone you're mean!!!!
With your heads held high,
you all stand proud, and
you want to "kiss your
teammate"!
Show the world we are
"superstars" – or we'll
quickly know our fate!

But let us look to the
future – as we all have
had enough.
What the England football
team really needs is; ' a
manager like Sir Brian
Clough.'
So, hail, hail, and hail
again, will England win
the day?
Only if they are managed
by; 'the ghost of Sir Alf
Ramsay.'

THE WORLD CUP COULD
BE AN ALIEN NATION

The World Cup is a trophy
that every player wants to
win,
Even if it means kicking a
player – right on his already
bruised shin!
It is a trophy of solid Gold –
and is loved by every player,
Every four years it arrives –
the football world's in top
gear!

Many nations do compete –
the prize awaits the best.
Playing in the groups they
do – the ultimate playing
test.
From all around the globe –
country's do compete,
All the world class players –
running on their feet.

From South America – to
Europe too – and even in
another galaxy,
The world cup finals are
watched in space – by an
alien large society!
Yes, my friends, Star Trek
is out there – they love the

U.S. soccer –
Together they watch in outer
space – it couldn't get any
better!

The world cup is a dream –
as the martians do enjoy;
'They play the game of
football – like it is a toy!'
Even the Champions League –
is known in outer space,
The martians are so very
skillful – they admire the
human race.

The space is in total darkness,
but there's a match being
played tonight,
Is it the martian' World Cup –
or a "Trick or Treat" delight?
Our game of football is now
known – even in deepest
space;
'The martians enjoy our world
cup – as we play with so much
grace.'

So, as the world teams do
battle – for a prize of glory,
Is the space game so surreal –
or just another story?
The World Cup and the
Champions League – are all
prestige' sporting competitions,
Even if we're being watched –

by martian's from an alien-
being' space galaxy nations!!!!

THE GOLDEN BOOT OF
FOOTBALL AWARD

The golden boot of football,
is given only to a select few,
So if you surely want one –
you must now join a queue.
This award is an honour –
and it salutes the player's
ability,
The golden football boot
award – is also internationally.

The golden football boot
ward – is a prize to hold
and cherish,
The only thing you cannot
do is smother the boot in
polish!
Every player drools, and
would love to own this boot –
But you really have to be
exceptional – and wear a
very smart suit.

It really is a privilege to
hold up high this award,
Everyone does want it – but
you have to be a soccer
lord.
The golden football boot,
is a special prize for sure,
Only the cream of the crop,

can feel the boot's amour.

So let us see the players –
who tend to win this as a
big surprise.
When they lift the golden
boot – tears do fill their eyes.
From England through to
the Europe greats – and also
far and wide,
Every football player in the
world today – this football
boot we abide.

So, who will seek this golden
boot out – and cherish it
for ever?
Whoever is awarded it – it
will be their true endeavour.
From world cup greats – the
list is there – all the players'
now on board:
'Ladies and gentleman I ask
you now – who'll win the
golden football boot award?'

THE MAGIC OF A TIMELESS
ENGLISH LANDMARK

The football players I see at the Wembley Stadium,
looking so splendour,
It invites me to look closer –
the magic I will capture?
The stadium is so awesome,
it feels fit for a king,
And when I move even
closer – I even start to sing!

I see the Wembley Stadium,
it really does look grand,
I have to get even closer –
and listen to the band.
It is a fabulous stadium, as
legend already knows,
The home of internationals –
and where the fans all roars.

The magic Wembley Stadium,
is a sight to behold,
Many teams have been
privileged – a story to be told?
England have played there –
and also Scotland, too,
Even Wales and Ireland – all
are in the queue!

All the world class teams have
graced this awesome stadium,
Brazil and also Germany –

and Holland is the spectrum.
South America are also there –
with Argentina and Chile,
All have played at Wembley –
a privilege of duty.

So the magic that is Wembley,
the stadium of football,
You may get the chance to
play there – but you have to
score a goal!
From Wembley Stadium, we
welcome you – to watch these
world class teams,
Where you can see the stars
in action – and not only in your
dreams.

knew – were the cream of
the crop.
And when they went on the
pitch – we'd see who came
out on top?
I remember Francis Lee,
and Mike Summerbee,
Then came Colin Bell,
who all played for
Manchester City.

Even the Arsenal – now
they also were the stunners.
From Charlie George – to
Pat Jennings – they were
the brilliant' Gunners!

71

At Highbury they played –
every match an epic,
Even their manager –
George Graham was a
tonic!

Leeds United were also
there, all dressed in
virginal white.
All their brilliant players –
a magical delight.
From Billy Bremner, to
Peter Lorimar – and Allan
Clarke, too,
They really were a dynamic
team – one heck of a crew!

All the teams of the golden
years – so many I could
name,
They all played so brilliant –
at their chosen game.
Kevin Keegan and John
Toshack – and also Jimmy
Greaves,
They all were simply
superb – they had magic
up their sleeves!!!!

And even when it was
snowing – the lads would
all stall play,
They ran about all over the
place – they simply enjoyed

their day.
The fans all cheered – and
some really swore,
But everyone enjoyed
themselves – then a player
would often score!!!!

The magic days out at the
football match, really was a
treat,
The players all entertaining
us – the ball was at their
feet.
The final whistle was then
blown, and everyone just
cheered,
Then before the arrival of
health and safety – the
grounds were carefully
cleared.

The golden years of the
football teams – and the

football players,
We idolised all the greats –
and we even shed some
tears!
Now we move forward to
a whole new generation –
and start a new found
nation;
'What a fabulous sport we
do have – our football
team's creation?'

THE FOOTBALL PLAYERS
THAT I ONCE KNEW

The football players I once
knew – were the cream of
the crop.
And when they went on the
pitch – we'd see who came
out on top?
I remember Francis Lee,
and Mike Summerbee,
Then came Colin Bell,
who all played for
Manchester City.

Even the Arsenal – now
they also were the stunners.
From Charlie George – to
Pat Jennings – they were
the brilliant' Gunners!
At Highbury they played –
every match an epic,
Even their manager –
George Graham was a
tonic!

Leeds United were also
there, all dressed in
virginal white.
All their brilliant players –
a magical delight.
From Billy Bremner, to
Peter Lorimar – and Allan

Clarke, too,
They really were a dynamic
team – one heck of a crew!

All the teams of the golden
years – so many I could
name,
They all played so brilliant –
at their chosen game.
Kevin Keegan and John
Toshack – and also Jimmy
Greaves,
They all were simply
superb – they had magic
up their sleeves!!!!

And even when it was
snowing – the lads would
all stall play,
They ran about all over the
place – they simply enjoyed
their day.
The fans all cheered – and
some really swore,
But everyone enjoyed
themselves – then a player
would often score!!!!

The magic days out at the
football match, really was a
treat,
The players all entertaining
us – the ball was at their
feet.

The final whistle was then
blown, and everyone just
cheered,
Then before the arrival of
health and safety – the
grounds were carefully
cleared.

The golden years of the
football teams – and the
football players,
We idolised all the greats –
and we even shed some
tears!
Now we move forward to
a whole new generation –
and start a new found
nation;
'What a fabulous sport we
do have – our football
team's creation?'

BECKS TO THE FUTURE

'Father dear,' said Romeo in
2022,
'What team shall I play for,
Now I'm grown like you?
Should I play for Real Madrid
Or should it be Manyou?'

Why not play for Crewe?'
Mrs Becks walked in and
said:
'Why not play for who?'

'Oh my gosh,' said Becks to
Posh,
'I thought you were in Venice.'
'I was, but now I'm back in
Britain
For a game of tennis.'

'Mother dear,' said Romeo,
'Sit down with us here.
The three of us can now
discuss
My footballing career.

'Now tell me, my dear parents,
If I play in attack
'What number should be printed
On the Beckham back?'

'Well my little angel,
If you want to play in Heaven
'Where your father's dreams were
made,

Why not number seven?'

'But mother dear,' said Romeo,
'When father off to Spain did flee
'In Madrid, what Daddy did
was wear a twenty – three.'

Mrs Becks and Romeo
both looked round at Daddy.
It was Mrs B who spoke
and uttered to her hubby:

'David let us know, the number,
that you recommend for our dear
Romeo.'
David Beckham cleared his throat
and croaked those words we've
grown to know:

'Wear Four out there, Romeo.'

SUCKING ON MY THUMB
SCORING FOR THE HAMMERS

I am a Premier League footballer –
and sometime's I feel numb,
And every time I score a goal –
I tend to suck my thumb!
I play for West Ham United, also
known as 'the Hammers',
But when I start to suck my
thumb – my team mates get
the jitters!!

I must admit it makes a change
from all the constant snogging;
'So as I now suck my thumb –
I've also started jogging!'
It takes me back to nursery
school – when I was just a
child,
Every time I sucked my thumb –
it drove the nurses wild!!

Even on the playing pitch – and
the weather is oh so shocking,
I'd tend to run about too much –
showing off my skin-tight
stocking!
We would also carry our mobile
phones – and send a text to our
girlfriends,
But when I'm sucking on my
thumb – I'm starting brand new

trends!

I play my football skillfully – and
we have a lot of fun,
And then in the winter – I jet
off to get some sun.
I fly to warmer climates – as the
UK's cold numbs my bum,
But I always will feel much
better – when I'm sucking on
my thumb!!!!

My name is Dimitri Payet, and
I play for West Ham United,
I scored two great wonder
goals – and got so very excited.
I started celebrating – and my
team mates grabbed my bum,
And all that excitement – it made
me suck my thumb!!!!

THE FOOTBALL WORLD HELPS
THE REFUGEES

We are the refugees, we
really need your assistance,
We are fleeing persecution –
as we sail to a new existence.
We are leaving our danger
land – it is known as
Syria –
Our lives have all been torn
apart – causing mass hysteria.

But, wait, there's breaking
news; 'a land of football
stars',
They are playing football
and some do play guitars!
The Europe teams have
united – and their aim is
charity –
To help all the poor people –
known as a refugee.

Even the English Premier
League – they too are raising
money,
To help us to our new life –
on our perilous journey.
From Liverpool to Everton,
from Bournemouth and also
Chelsea,
We also love Manchester
United – and their rivals –

Manchester City!

They along with Barcelona –
and Real Madrid together,
Inter Milan and A.C. Milan –
they always get good
weather!
The fantastic teams we
all do see – is a treat for us
all, so please;
'Thank you from our hearts
and souls – as we are the
football refugees.'

A TRIBUTE TO BOTH SIR
BOBBY CHARLTON AND
WAYNE ROONEY

Wayne Rooney has equalled
a record, and made football
history,
He equalled his England goal
scoring – to add to his own
tally.
This record was previously
held by Sir Bobby Charlton,
And what did seem to Rooney,
it must have been a marathon!

Both of these players have
links to Manchester United,
And both of these super
players – their goals were so
invited.
The brilliant Sir Bobby Charlton,
he played for a super team,
The players of years gone by –
they really were a dream.

But Manchester United have
struggled so of late,
Was the goal by Wayne Rooney –
seen as football fate?
Rooney is a different player –
that is evident –
Bobby Charlton was world class –
he really was a gent!

The players of today – no matter
what their team,
Playing in the England football
team – is their biggest dream.
Back in the 1970s – and the 1980s,
footballers never wore gloves,
Except for the goalkeeper – they
really took the shoves!

Wayne Rooney is the highest
goal scorer – that is now the
case,
But being the all time England's
best player – Sir Bobby Charlton
was real ace!
Sir Bobby has one achievement –
which Wayne Rooney will never
better,
Sir Bobby Charlton won the world
cup – and he has this title forever.

But, well done anyway – to the
footballer Wayne Rooney,
He hangs on in there – and collects
his loadsa money!!!!
I think the world cup will always
evade the England team,
But, congratulations to Wayne
Rooney; 'you've achieved your
perfect dream.'

MANCHESTER UNITED: THE
RED DEVILS OF YESTERYEAR

We really love our football
and we watch it on TV,
We like to watch the English
Premier League – but sadly
it isn't free!
The top teams are in action –
and they show a lot of skill,
But they don't like playing
in Winter time in case they
catch a chill!

Let's go back some decades
and marvel at some players,
Bobby Charlton played midfield –
and he could strike the ball so
fierce.
Then came George Best, he
never liked to train –
He was always down the pub –
his drinking did remain.

Dennis Law came along – and
he also played for Man City,
Scoring a crafty goal – which
he really did so pity.
He was a Scot and he could
play – he was the prodigal son,
But that crafty little back-heel –
sent United to Division One!

Then came Sir Alex Ferguson –
he was a canny Scot,
He had all the best players in
sight – so he bought the blinking
lot!
He was so very successful, this
we can't deny,
But if he ever lost a game – he'd
give a little sigh!

He also conquered Europe, just
like the Busby babes,
Winning every trophy there –
and he never wore his shades!
His mouth would rotate a lot –
and more trophy's were to come,
Thanks to his winning style – and
his beloved chewing gum!!!!

Sir Alex has now retired – and Van
Gaal is now the manager –
Trying his best to win the games –
with Ryan Giggs, his deputy mentor.
They have been very busy – in
the signings of new players,
But missing out on a player –
that turned them all to jeers!!!!

We really love our football – that
is very clear,
Watching them run around – and
never show any fear!
The English Premier League – is
where the action is –

But don't forget the Champions
League – for it too is really BLISS!

FOOTBALL IS A GAME...
SIMPLY OUT OF THIS
WORLD

The planets float around all
day – within the outer space,
They sometimes chat and
watch TV – they do this so
with grace.
They've discovered a new
interest – which really does
intrigue,
They get together every
week – and watch the English
Football Premier League!

These planets have been so
dormant – but they discovered
a magic moment,
They were told of the English
Premier League – so they
checked out this installment!
They saw the angels all sat
down – watching Real Madrid –
They shouted and they clapped
their wings – just as all the
humans did!

Then the planets got a TV –
made by Panasonic,
They then started to watch
the football – and the teams
were really magic.

The planets were all so
amazed – and while watching
Barcelona –
When Barcelona scored a goal,
they shouted: 'HALLELUJHA!'

All the angels and the planets
had never seen this before,
They were watching European
football – 'oh, what a score!!!!'
The universe was all lit up –
as the planets lit up their lights,
And all the angels sat with
them – to watch the football
highlights!

They really were all cheering –
and the planets were so
excited,
'This game of earthling football –
is really very good – and we'll
have to watch Man United!
So every Saturday, they all
gathered round – like something
out of Star Trek;
'And watched all the European
football – the results they did
so check.'

These planets are also very
thrilled with the brilliant' Inter
Milan,
Watching them play in the
their space galaxy – everything

goes to plan.
The planets tell the angels – of
these fabulous new teams,
And when the magic floodlights
shine – you can see them in
your dreams.

From Saturn, Earth and Neptune,
and Mars soon follows suit,
Jupiter is also there – eating juicy
fruit!
The planets have now discovered –
a truly remarkable game,
From the European super teams –
all do make their name.

A new galaxy of planet stars – are
shining in the sky,
The planets are watching the football –
the English Premier League, so high.
The magic is all there – and the planets
are all so thrilled –
The super European football leagues –
their skill is now distilled.

The game of football and soccer, has
reached outer space,
The planets are so impressed – they
even do say grace!
When the games have ended – and
they meet their perfect hosts;
'The planets are now introduced – to
the brilliant O-Posts.'
So welcome to the game of football –

as the planets all shout; 'HOORAY!'
'Thank you so very much – and we'll
see you all on Saturday!!!!'

WELCOME TO WEST HAM...
UP THE HAMMERS

My name is Alf Garnett,
and I'm married to a
silly moo,
Every day I get up – she
tells me what to do!
I am a big West Ham
United fan – (up the
hammers!),
I follow them where-
ever they go – oh, I give
some lectures!!

I go to watch them play –
and I sometimes use
my wheelchair,
I ask Merrigold to push
me – because he's paid
to care?
I do like to rant a lot –
and the West Ham shirt,
I will wear,
I can't control my
emotions – I always
have to swear!!

I also like the England –
when they won in 1966 –
Some say we were lucky –
some say it was a fix!!!!
I have my Sunday lunch,
and watch the TV soccer,

But, my irate wife is doing
the ironing – I really
should help her!!

But, I have to get ready –
to go and watch West
Ham –
I get sick and very tired –
of travelling on a tram.
I have to make this
journey – ever single week,
Then I have to queue at
the match – they have a
bloody cheek!!

Once I am there – I sit in
the disabled area,
I keep a watchful eye out –
the stewards are always
there.
If I use my wheelchair –
and take Marigold, as well,
He's always prancing
around the place – he
really makes me yell!!

So, welcome to the
hammers – and West Ham
United,
You can all come in – but
only if your invited!!
Come and sit next to me –
and my carer – Marigold,
Enjoy the game – and

the win – well, this is what
I'm told!!!!

THOSE CLASSY PLAYERS...
WHO GRACE THE
ENGLISH PREMIER LEAGUE

We are the super football
clubs, and we play in the
English Premier League,
We are the elite of our
game – together, we do
intrigue.
We pride ourselves on
skill – for that there is no
doubt,
When we score a goal –
or two – the fans really
do shout.

We also entertain you –
as you do pay very good
money,
You sit in the stands in
the sun – also in pure
luxury.
We value you as our
supporters – that is very
true,
We will put on a super
game – especially for
you.

We run about all over
the pitch – we pass the
ball with ease,

With the fans all cheering –
we are just eager to please.
Families come and enjoy
the game – and children
all do cheer,
When half-time does arrive –
some adults enjoy a beer!

These teams are all
professional – they entertain
the fans,
Cheering, shouting and
dancing – it all happens in
the stands.
The atmosphere is superb,
and everyone is so happy,
Even a family sitting down –
they have a 'laughing' baby!

Saturday's are very special –
we love our football games,
Some of us go every week –
even naming all the names!
There is a shop you can go
to – to buy a football
programme,
Even a tasty sandwich –
tomato and some ham!

You can also buy a hot snack,
pie and peas is tasty,
Or a hot cheesy toasty – or
a delicious Cornish Pasty!
Hot drinks are also available –

to tempt your pallet more;
'From OXO, through to Bovril –
hot soup we all do adore.'

The fans come from
everywhere, just to watch
us play,
We always do entertain them,
in our own unique way.
The super stars are on display –
all of whom intrigue;
'Those classy, world class
players – who grace the
English Premier League.'

A WORLD CLASS PLAYER...
A PREMIER LEAGUE STAR

The Premier League, is
the league so great,
The stars come out –
with ball at feet,
Classy players, is what
they are,
Some will play a fine
guitar.

Running round the pitch
they do,
Never standing in any
queue,
Playing tricks with a
football now,
Now they go for their
chow.

They are first class – that
is true,
Playing for the privileged
few,
Sounds of; 'GOAL!' Come
to light,
It really is, a pure delight.

Please pass the ball to
me I ask?
I've got my lunch – and

my flask,
Even now the team do
play,
And some of us – will
now pray.

Where's my shorts, they
have got lost?
I need them now – I
blame Jack Frost!
It's freezing cold – I'm
not impressed,
The football game – is
now addressed.

We are all united – that's
for sure,
Winning more – we all
adore.
Kissing is a joy to see,
Then come and sit –
upon my knee!!!!

We are now ready, for
the match,
The World Cup Final –
where's the catch?
We're very proud – and
glory be,
Now we play – on live
TV.

All the teams are there

to see,
Entry now, for you is FREE.
The excitement grows,
here we go –
Come along to a soccer
show.

The world does watch,
as we all now play,
Hoping for a good display.
Italian players – and Spanish
too –
They're the best – of the
chosen few.

Come along and meet
your host,
The delightful team of
the O-Post.
Goal by goal – they will
bring you –
All the transfers – are
in the queue.

Settle down and rejoice
with me –
To watch the skills of
those you see,
The Premier League – is
the league,
Full of stars – and all
intrigue!

Here we go it's time
to play,
Watching now – it's a-okay.
Forever soccer – is what
we are,
A world class player –
a Premier League Star.

THE SKY SPORTS BLUES

Sky Sports now have
increased their prices,
All this and more – it's
no surprises,
Inflation leaps up to
the sky,
High prices – they can't
deny.

The Sky Sports team
know their football,
They commentate in
their own bubble.
Talking football – and
earning their pay,
All this and more – on
Saturday.

Jeff Stelling and friends,
they start new trends,
Reporting on games –
till the ends.
Former footballers –
do take part,
They're so very
passionate – right from
the heart.

Sky Sports do cover,
the Europe' too,
All this and more – just

for you.
Champions League – is
also there,
The World Cup hopes –
if we dare!

The Europe League's are
also great,
They are super skilled –
the fans create?
The FA Cup – Sky Sports
will cover,
I don't know why the
BBC do bother!!!!

The Sky Sports team still
sing the blues,
Cos no Premier League
team' likes to lose.
They chat and laugh at
each other,
The Sky Sports team…
the ball's in their quarter!

Just keep on watching
the Sky TV,
But you'll have to pay –
it isn't for free!
The Sky Sports Blues –
is what we all hear,
When a goal is scored –
there is a loud cheer!

So pull up a chair and
sit and cheer,
Eat some crisps – and
have a cold beer!!
The Sky Sports Blues
is the song to choose.
Because no Premier
League team likes to
lose!!!!

WELCOME TO OUR TEAM...
THE FIRST GAY MALE
FOOTBALLER

The football world is now
changing – something is
being revealed,
Something which will
make history – both on
and off the field.

For decades it has been
known – but no one dare
come out –
For fear of persecution –
and everyone would
shout?

The world of male football –
will change now, and for
ever,
True feelings are coming
out – we are now all
together.

"What am I talking about,
you ask me so politely?
The element of change,
my friends – for a whole
new sexuality."

The men's sport will now
feature – the first ever
gay man,
This will change the way
we play – accept it? Yes,
we can!

The first gay footballer –
is making history,
No more hiding away –
coming out to be free.

Welcome to the 21st
century – and we all
welcome this change
to be.
There's nothing wrong
with a gay footballer –
we welcome you with
glee.

The team accepts this
news – and smiles at
the star,
"Don't you worry, we
welcome you – now
you will go far."

More teams will follow
suit – as more players
come out as gay,
There's nothing to be
ashamed of – we love

you either way?

Everyone is happy – as
the gay footballer is now
here,
And when the full time
whistle blows – we can
enjoy a nice cold beer!!!!

All the bigotry is in the
past – and that is history,
For every footballer is
so equal – and that is
plain to see.

Hallelujha, I know this
now – and every man
is equal –
From footballers – to
the referee – the game
is now on schedule.

Everyone's the same –
no one is any different,
Now we play our football –
and enjoy the crowd
excitement.

Congratulations is for
sure – as barriers are
broke down.
From gay men – to
straight men – we all

wear one crown.

The world has now
made history – and
we salute it every year.
Please welcome to our
football team – the
'first gay football player.

LOVE ME TENDER...
LOVE MY FOOTBALL

Love me tender, love
my football, tell me you
are mine,
For it's you that I do
love – and our hearts
entwine.
Love me tender, love
football – we are the
elite,
Welcome to the Premier
League, we don't
accept defeat.

Chorus:
Love me tender, we love
you – we mean that oh
so true,
For our O-Posts are
always there – we rely
on you.

Love me tender, I do
play, this is my home
league,
For you have been
good to me – creating
such intrigue.
Love me tender, love
football – we are the
champions –
For my darling I love

111

you – the darling soccer
nations,

Chorus:
Chorus:
Love me tender, love
our game, this is what
we do,
For our darling football
team – you are the
special few.

Love me tender, love
the sport, the light is
shining bright.
We are playing at
home today – we do
feel such delight.
Love us tender, love
the sport – for we can't
always win,
For my darlings we
will win – and this is
not a sin!

Chorus:
Love my footy, love
my team, you really
are a dream.
For on the pitch you
do deliver – and
cause us all to scream.

Love me tender, love

the ref, for he is in
full charge.
He is always booking
us – for a foul of a
shoulder barge.
Love him tender, love
his style, the ref is
like a thistle,
When he retires from
the game – he'll blow
the final whistle.

Chorus:
Love me tender, love
football, the O-Posts
team are great.
They are up to date
for us – this we
appreciate.

Love me tender, I'm
in love – with the
skills of the modern
game.
All the players we
do see – but I do
not know their name.
Love me tender, love
football – it is a very
rich sport,
When you run out on
to the pitch – the ball
is in your court.

113

Chorus:
Love me tender, love
the dream – we really
are the host.
The world's best league's
are all on show, thanks
to our O-Posts.

Love me tender, we
love bath time, who's
now pinched the soap?
If we score some goals
today – we can all elope.
Love me tender, love us
true, this football we all
do play,
Never wondering why
we play – except for our
massive pay!

WE'RE FOOTBALL CRAZY...
WE'RE FOOTBALL MAD

Blue is the colour, Chelsea
is the team,
Then comes Everton – all
within a dream.
We're football crazy – we're
football mad,
And if our team do lose
again – we'll be so very
mad!

Red is the colour, Liverpool
are now mean,
Then comes the Arsenal,
somewhere in between!
We're football potty, we're
football loopy,
Welcome to Highbury, and
Anfield for your duty?

Winning is the order, losing
we do hate,
But every week we play our
game – it really is our fate.
Yellow is the colour, Leeds
are up there too,
So are Norwich City – those
canaries take their pew!

Then the half time whistle,

it blows now for half time,
We have to go to the shop –
and lots of stairs we climb!
Some people now are having
a drink – their throats are
very dry,
But that's not surprising –
when you're eating a nice
meat pie!!!!

Now it's back to the game –
but now I've lost my seat,
Someone has just scored a
goal – and I believe it was a
treat!!!!
I'm football crazy – I'm
football mad –
Now it is home time – I feel
so very sad.

Shouting as we go – and
waving our arms about,
Singing our beloved team –
to a rocking' twist and
shout!!!!
We also love our football –
and our dear old wives,
But only on a Saturday –
when they act like Dr
Phibes!!!!

Let's all sing together – as
footy is our dream,
Singing songs of football –

praising all the team.
Now we are so happy – now
to rest a while,
Let's all go to Blackpool Town –
and see the Golden Mile!!!!

THE BRILLIANT LIVERPOOL
PLAYERS OF YESTERYEAR
AND ANFIELD

We were the greatest Liverpool
team to ever grace the pitch,
We really were the kings of the
Kop – and all without a glitch.
We wore the red shirt of pride –
a very proud honour –
We always played majestically,
complimenting each other.

The Anfield team really were
supreme – we were feared by
all the rest.
Every match day on the Kop –
the fans – they were the best.
The cheers from the kop – was
unlike any other,
All the family's all did come –
and they all…'watched with
mother!'

The players too – they were
supreme – and they knew how
to pass the ball.
Tackling as they went along –
listening for the call?
Those awesome defenders –
protecting their goalkeeper,
Brilliant in their role – possibly
the saviour!

Kevin Keegan he was great,
he also played for England,
Emlyn Hughes had the blues,
they really are now legend.
Steve Heighway, he was there –
gliding down the wing,
Terry McDermott and Graham
Sounes – also did their thing.

They even had a 'super-sub'
who liked to call their bluff,
He always came on as a sub –
their saviour…David Fairclough.
Their goalkeeper was a gem –
he would always save them,
The ever reliable' Ray Clemence,
he jumped and dived in mayhem!!

One thing they had in common –
was their title' heir,
Also in the 70s – they all had curly
permed hair!
They played in all types of weather,
even in the snow.
They didn't wear woolen gloves –
real men you have to know!!

They really were the champions –
of Europe and the UK –
But unlike the boys today – they
didn't get very good pay!
They played for the love of the

game – that is very true,
And every Saturday at Anfield –
they played a game for you.

Kenny Dalglish was a player –
also a manager,
He came from Bonny Scotland –
he really was their saviour.
Joe Fagan was a sensation – a
manager, precisely.
Also in the same class – was
the brilliant Bob Paisley.

The managers of bygone years,
were all stars to know,
They all graced the Liverpool
shirt – their skills were all on
show.
But the legend of them all – a
brilliant man, honestly,
He commanded all respect –
the one and only…BILL SHANKLY.

The Liverpool team of the past –
like others – were a super team
to watch,
And every match-day in the bathtub –
they liked a drop of Scotch!!
The true greats of Liverpool – are
in our memory, far afield.
Welcome to the home of the
Liverpool…the brilliant ANFIELD.

THE MIGHTY LEEDS UNITED...
PLAYERS OF YESTERYEAR

Billy Bremner had a temper,
which was plain to see,
And if you tried to tackle
him – he'd kick you on your
knee!

There was also Peter Lorimar,
if he came at you, you'd
know it,
He also had a lethal right
foot – a shot just like a bullet!

Joe Jordan was a Scot, a fiery
one at that,
If you ever crossed him – his
fists would knock you flat!

There was even Jack Charlton –
and his brother, Bobby –
They both played for England,
alongside little' Nobby!

Then came Allan Clarke, a
quiet man, we gather,
He scored a winning FA Cup
goal – with a diving header.

Don Revie was the manager –
of the brilliant, Leeds United.
Now they are all in the past –
and some have now departed!

Leeds United, all in white –
were feared by most teams,
Trying their best to win the
game – if only in their dreams!

Now I end my journey – a
trip back in time,
A tribute to Leeds United
players, in a 'poetic' little rhyme.

THE AMAZING WORLD OF
FOOTBALL TRANSFERS

The transfer news does
now amuse, big money
is paid on time,
Although many object –
is what we expect, it
really isn't a crime.

The agents are there –
and they do car, what
will the offer be?
A fee so big – you have
a jig – now you are
so free.

Sky Sports are there,
BT beware, to buy the
Premier League rights,
The highest bidder – is
the one that's quicker,
please, hold on to your
tights!!!!

The players are all world
class – vast fortunes
they all do amass,
They play so supreme, it
does seem a dream, they
really are sheer class.

Wheeling and dealings,
are seen as the trimmings,
the transfers are now on
the table,
So go with the flow, as you
all well know – the game is
now all stable.

With a dollar to spare, I
really do care – as I fly
across the Atlantic,
To see LA Galaxy, is my
own fantasy – it really
is pure magic.

Steven Gerrard is there, with
out any care, with Frank
Lampard – they now will go
far.
To play soccer in style,
they've waited a while –
in America – they are now
a big star.

The transfers are done – and
the football's begun, the stars
are set to do battle,
The Champions League – and
the English Premier League,
will now do battle as traditional.

CHELSEA SING THE BLUES...
WINNING GAMES IS WHAT
WE CHOOSE

We are the boys in blue,
and we are the ones to
trust,
When we march on to
the pitch – watching our
skill is a must.
We are the Chelsea elite,
we play at Stamford
Bridge,
And we are the defending
champions – because we
have the courage.

We won the Premier League,
in the summer of 2014,
Now we are defending it –
do you know what I mean?
We have a great defender,
the brilliant, John Terry,
We also had Frank Lampard –
but he went to Man City.

We have a wealthy owner,
and a flamboyant manager,
Known as the "SPECIAL"
one – he always hides his
anger!
Jose Mourinho is his name –
and he comes from Portugal,

Wanting to win ever game –
it is his football will!!

There even is Drogba, Ashley
Cole' as well,
Together as a strike force –
they really do so gel.
Lots of others too – all the
best right now,
When they parade on the
pitch – all the fans do bow.

The Chelsea boys are now
all ready – but, who do you
choose?
Even in the dressing room –
Chelsea sings the blues!!!!
So, good luck to the blues,
and Chelsea' is their name,
And winning the English
Premier League, is their
one true aim.

ARSENAL FOREVER...
WE ARE THE MIGHTY
ARSENAL

We are the mighty Arsenal –
we are a world-class team,
We play our game so
majestically, we really are
supreme.

We play in the English Premier
League – and we fear no
other team,
Not even Manchester United –
do you know what I mean?

Highbury is our home – we
also recruit beginners,
Our famous name is known
to all – we are the world-
class GUNNERS.

We really do have a history –
of famous players in time,
All were simply brilliant –
they really were sublime.

There was goalkeeper, Bob
Wilson – and the manager,
George Graham,
Every match they played –
it was a jam-packed stadium.

The most important game
they played in – was a classic'

FA Cup Final,
When Charlie George let
loose a shot – it really was
unstoppable.

But now they soldier on –
with a super manager,
And they continue to be
a world-class team, Arsenal –
forever.

THE ENGLISH PREMIER
LEAGUE KICK-OFF

The Premier League has
now kicked off – we can
now applaud the players,
Walking on to the perfect
pitch – showing off their
kickers.
Boots all gleaming white –
and on occasions – shiny
yellow,
And if a footballer goes
up to the crowd – it's just
to say; 'HELLO?'

Out of the tunnel they
proudly march,
With their shirts and
shorts all ironed with
starch.
Fans all singing – as
they stand in a line –
All singing loudly – so
divine.

The referee is there –
looking so stern and
manly,
He has a pocket smart
phone – and listens to
Accrington Stanley!!
The referee's assistants –
stand and run the pitch,

All this and a lot more –
but sometimes there's a
glitch!!

The elite teams are all
in action – playing for
their lives,
Each player knowing –
only one survives!!
There can only be one
winner – or a score draw,
is an option,
When these top players
play – they really show
devotion.

So, welcome to the
home – of the English
Premier teams,
All of them knowing –
winning is their dreams.
So grab the remote
control – and settle down
to view,
The English Premier
League – is now here –
for me and for you!!

ENGLAND'S WORLD CUP
MISERY

The World Cup Finals
we aim at – every four
long years,
But with the current
England team – it
always ends in tears!
No matter how we try –
or who the manager
is –
We always fail to
qualify – and we lose
on penalties!!

We used to be so
good – and we won
almost everything,
England's brave lion-
hearts – cannot win
anything!
Please excuse my
cynicism, I'd love to
be more positive –
But with the shabby
performances – of
the England's negative?

We seem to lack
the talent – and some
just don't qualify,
We never win anything –
it really makes us cry!!

England used to be –
the very best of all,
Walking out onto the
pitch – all feeling ten
foot tall!!

Even the European
Championships – we
never do any good,
And we have "world
class" players – as we
darn well should!!
We have got some
brilliant players – but
many are from over-
seas,
We don't have much
home-grown talent –
who can win for
England – with ease!!

And, why are they
always spitting? This
is so very dirty.
Running around
slobbering – getting
rather shirty!!
Maybe in the future –
England will reign
supreme,
Well, yes, I know, but
I can pray – if only in a
dream!!!!

WELCOME TO THE CAPTIVATING WORLD OF ENGLISH FOOTBALL

Welcome to the Premier
League – it is a world
away,
A league were all the
soccer players – get
very high pay.
The Arsenal, and the
Chelsea – Spurs and
West Ham –
Are all in the city of
London – near the
Birmingham!

Then there's Manchester
City – competing with
Manchester United,
These two play a mean
old game – and are now
so well divided.
Little Blackpool were in
a dream – and played the
top notch teams,
But, sadly, they got
relegated – the end of
all their dreams!

Fleetwood Town and
Accrington too – they

both played like silk,
Especially little Accrington –
by drinking plenty of
milk!!
Fleetwood will play
Blackpool – in Division
One –
Who will win this derby
match – and be the
prodigal son?

It isn't just about the
big boys – who are in
the top flight clubs,
But winning lots of
games you play –
depends on your good
subs!!!
The managers are there –
and they talk, shout
and scream,
Winning every game
they play – is their only
dream.

So, here we go again, to
a brand new soccer
season,
All the football clubs are
there – and all have very
good reason.
The Premier League, the
Championship – there's
Division One, too,
If any of them keep losing

games – they'll end up in
Division Two!!!!

THE WORLD OF ENGLISH
FOOTBALL AND USA
SOCCER

The football season
is now reborn,
The kissing of the
players – is now the
norm.
They score a goal –
and scream like a
woman –
They also dance –
as their erotica is
awoken!!

They run around on
a pitch –
Stopping only – to
wipe their snitch.
Over paid – and
messing around,
In the dressing
room – they pace
the ground.

The world of soccer –
in the USA –
All the boys all come
out and play.
They have just signed
David Beckham –
Followed by Steven
Gerrard – a scouser'

they reckon!!

Diving they do – it's
now their culture,
Conning the ref – is
it any wonder?
But the kissing they
do – and it doesn't
look nice,
Are they behaving –
like they're running
a vice?

The English Premier
League, it is so very
rich,
Loads of talent – or,
is it a glitch?
Sky Sports and BT –
have paid over the
odds,
Raising my phone
line rental – the
greedy sods!!!!

Welcome to soccer –
in the USA –
Where everyone is
happy – come what
may!
So enjoy your football –
and feel the bliss;
'If you do score a goal –
do you have to kiss?'

27163347R00077

Printed in Great Britain
by Amazon